**Stepping into Standards
Theme Series**

Habitats

Written by
Heather D. Phillips

Editors: Pamela Jennett and Sheri Rous
Illustrator: Darcy Tom
Cover Illustrators: Darcy Tom and Kimberly Schamber
Designer: Moonhee Pak
Cover Designer: Moonhee Pak
Art Director: Tom Cochrane
Project Director: Carolea Williams

Table of Contents

Introduction

Due to the often-changing national, state, and district standards, it is frequently difficult to "squeeze in" fascinating topics for student enrichment on top of meeting required standards and including a balanced program in your classroom curriculum. The *Stepping into Standards Theme Series* incorporates required subjects and skills for second- and third-grade students while engaging them in an exciting and meaningful theme. Students will participate in a variety of language arts experiences to help them with **reading** and **writing** skills. They will also enjoy **standards-based math activities, hands-on science projects,** and **interactive social studies activities.**

The creative lessons in *Habitats* provide imaginative, innovative ideas to help you motivate students as they learn about habitats in your classroom. The activities will inspire students to explore habitats as well as provide them with opportunities to enhance their knowledge and meet state standards. The pretest and posttest will help you assess your students' knowledge of the subject matter and skills.

Invite students to explore a variety of habitats as they
- learn about the different habitats and biomes of the world
- identify the living and nonliving parts of a habitat
- explore the interdependence of species with each other and their environment
- compare habitats, biomes, and ecosystems
- create a habitat for a particular animal
- create poems, stories, and illustrations that reflect knowledge about habitats

Each resource book in the *Stepping into Standards Theme Series* includes standards information, numerous activities, easy-to-use reproducibles, and a full-color overhead transparency to help you integrate a fun theme into your required curriculum. You will see how easy it can be to incorporate creative activities with academic requirements while students enjoy their exploration of habitats!

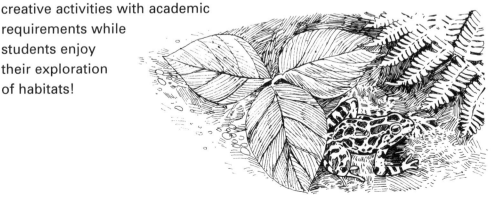

Getting Started

How to Use This Book

This comprehensive resource is filled with all the components you need to introduce, teach, review, and assess students on key skills while still making their learning experience as memorable as possible. The lessons are divided into four main sections: Language Arts, Math, Science, and Social Studies. Follow these simple steps to maximize student learning.

1 Use the **Meeting Standards** chart (pages 6–7) to help you identify the standards featured in each activity and incorporate them into your curriculum.

2 Review **Introducing . . . Habitats** (page 8). This page provides numerous facts about the theme of study, literature selections that work well with the theme, key vocabulary words that your students will encounter while studying the theme, and the answers to all the assessments presented throughout the resource. Use this page to obtain background knowledge and ideas to help you make this a theme to remember!

3 Use the **Habitats Pretest** (page 9) to assess your students' prior knowledge of the theme. This short, knowledge-based, multiple-choice test focuses on the key components of habitats. Use the results to help determine how much introduction to provide for the theme. The test can also be administered again at the end of the unit of study to see how much students have learned.

4 Copy the **What Do You Know? KWL Chart** (page 10) onto an overhead transparency, or enlarge it onto a piece of chart paper. Ask students to share what they already know about different habitats. Record student responses in the "What We **Know**" column. Ask students to share what they would like to know about habitats. Record student responses in the "What We **Want** to Know" column. Then, set aside the chart. Revisit it at the end of the unit. Ask students to share what they learned about habitats, and record their responses in the "What We **Learned**" column.

5 Give students the **Habitats—Reading Comprehension Test** (pages 11–12). It is a great way to introduce students to the theme while making learning interesting. You can assess your students' comprehension skills as well as introduce students to the components of habitats. The multiple-choice questions require students to use literal as well as inferential skills.

6 Use the **Parts of a Habitat full-color transparency** to enhance the theme. Display the transparency at any time during the unit to support the lessons and activities and to help reinforce key concepts about habitats.

7 Use the activities from the **Language Arts, Math, Science, and Social Studies sections** (pages 13–61) to teach students about habitats and to help them learn, practice, and review the required standards for their grade level. Each activity includes a list of objectives, a materials list, and a set of easy-to-follow directions. Either complete each section in its entirety before continuing on to the next section, or mix and match activities from each section.

8 Use the skills-based **Habitats Cumulative Test** (pages 62–63) to help you assess both what your students learned about the theme and what skills they acquired while studying the theme. It will also help you identify if students are able to apply learned skills to different situations. This cumulative test includes both multiple-choice questions and short-answer questions to provide a well-rounded assessment of your students' knowledge.

9 Upon completion of the unit, reward your students for their accomplishments with the **Certificate of Completion** (page 64). Students are sure to be eager to share their knowledge and certificate with family and friends.

Meeting Standards

Language Arts	This Is a Habitat (PAGE 13)	Habitat Mini-Book (PAGE 14)	Defining Habitats (PAGE 15)	Habitat Mix-Up (PAGE 16)	Habitat Homonyms (PAGE 16)	Habitat Information Posters (PAGE 17)	Animal Poetry (PAGE 18)	My Senses Tell Me (PAGE 19)	The Human Habitat (PAGE 20)	An Important Lesson (PAGE 21)	Letter to a Friend (PAGE 22)	Habitat ABCs (PAGE 23)
READING												
Comprehension		•				•						
Homonyms					•							
Interpret Information	•	•				•			•	•		•
Summarize Text		•				•						
Vocabulary Development	•	•	•	•								
WRITING												
Alphabetical Order												•
Descriptive Writing								•		•		
Editing										•	•	
Friendly Letters											•	
Nouns							•					
Poetry							•					
Prewriting and Organization						•				•		
Sentences										•	•	•
Verbs							•					

Meeting Standards

Math
Science
Social Studies

	Savanna Math (PAGE 33)	Patterns of the Desert (PAGE 34)	Kelp Forest Graphing (PAGE 35)	Early Bird Gets the Worm (PAGE 36)	Rain Forest Problem Solving (PAGE 37)	Habitat Hog (PAGE 38)	Creating a Habitat (PAGE 47)	The Food Chain Connection (PAGE 48)	Animals in Danger (PAGE 49)	Endangered Animal Education (PAGE 49)	Square-Yard Ecosystems (PAGE 50)	A Map of a Wetland (PAGE 54)	Where in the World? (PAGE 55)	Geography of a Forest (PAGE 56)	A Trip to the Arctic (PAGE 57)	A Home for Me (PAGE 58)
MATH																
Data Analysis and Probability			•	•												
Number and Operations			•		•	•										
Patterning		•														
Problem Solving	•		•		•	•										
Reasoning and Proof			•	•	•	•										
SCIENCE																
Characteristics of Organisms							•	•	•	•						
Investigation and Experimentation									•		•					
Life Cycles of Organisms							•	•	•							
Organisms and Their Environments							•	•	•	•	•	•	•		•	•
SOCIAL STUDIES																
Community															•	•
Economics															•	•
Mapping												•	•	•		

Introducing . . . Habitats

FACTS ABOUT HABITATS

- The natural home of a plant or an animal is called a habitat.

- Habitats provide food, water, shelter, and space.

- Many different species live in a habitat.

- An ecosystem refers to all the living things in a habitat and how they interact with the nonliving parts of the habitat.

- Energy transfers from living thing to living thing through food webs in an ecosystem.

- A biome is a collection of habitats worldwide that are similar in climate and vegetation.

- In a habitat or biome, all things are interrelated: plants and plants, plants and animals, and animals and animals.

- Humans can have an impact on a habitat.

ASSESSMENT ANSWERS

Habitats Pretest (PAGE 9)
1. *d* 2. *b* 3. *a* 4. *b* 5. *a* 6. *c* 7. *d* 8. *b*

Habitats—Reading Comprehension Test (PAGES 11–12)
1. *a* 2. *a* 3. *d* 4. *a* 5. *c* 6. *b*

Habitats Cumulative Test (PAGES 62–63)
1. *a* 2. *c* 3. *d* 4. *b* 5. *b* 6. *d* 7. *a* 8. *b* 9. *c* 10. *c* 11. *Answers may vary*
12. *Answers may vary*

LITERATURE LINKS

A House is a House for Me by Mary Ann Hoberman (Puffin)

Imagine Living Here: This Place is Cold by Vicki Cobb (Walker and Company)

Imagine Living Here: This Place is Dry by Vicki Cobb (Walker and Company)

Imagine Living Here: This Place is High by Vicki Cobb (Walker and Company)

Imagine Living Here: This Place is Wet by Vicki Cobb (Walker and Company)

The Important Book by Margaret Wise Brown (Harper and Row)

Welcome to the Green House by Jane Yolen (Scholastic)

What Is a Biome? by Bobbie Kalman (Crabtree Publishing)

Who Lives Here? by Rozanne Lanczak Williams (Creative Teaching Press)

The World Beneath Your Feet by Judith E. Rinard (National Geographic Society)

VOCABULARY

aquatic	biome
carnivore	climate
desert	ecosystem
environment	forest
grassland	habitat
herbivore	interdependence
omnivore	pollution
predator	prey
shelter	space
species	tundra

Name_____   Date_____

Habitats Pretest

Directions: Fill in the best answer for each question.

1 The natural home of a plant or animal is called a _____.

   ⓐ tent

   ⓑ lake

   ⓒ forest

   ⓓ habitat

2 True or False: A habitat contains only one or two kinds of plants or animals.

   ⓐ true

   ⓑ false

3 True or False: Habitats provide food, shelter, water, and space.

   ⓐ true

   ⓑ false

4 An herbivore is _____.

   ⓐ a plant that is an herb

   ⓑ an animal that eats only plants

   ⓒ an animal that eats only other animals

   ⓓ an animal that eats both plants and animals

5 Why are plants called producers?

   ⓐ They are able to make their own food.

   ⓑ They eat other living things.

   ⓒ They make movies.

   ⓓ They consume sunlight and oxygen.

6 What is a predator?

   ⓐ an animal that is hunted and killed by other animals

   ⓑ a plant that lives in water

   ⓒ an animal that hunts and kills other animals

   ⓓ an animal that eats plants

7 Which of the following shows a simple food chain?

   ⓐ lion → grass → gazelle

   ⓑ rabbit → water → berries

   ⓒ rattlesnake → rock → rabbit

   ⓓ eagle → mouse → oats

8 When a plant or an animal species is no longer living, we say that it is _____.

   ⓐ threatened

   ⓑ extinct

   ⓒ disappearing

   ⓓ endangered

What Do You Know? KWL Chart

What We Know	What We Want to Know	What We Learned

Name_____   Date_____

Habitats—Reading Comprehension Test

Directions: Read the story and then answer the six questions.

Every animal needs a home. A home is more than a building. The home of a living thing includes the area around it. The home of a living thing is more like a neighborhood that has everything it needs to survive. This "neighborhood" is called a habitat. A habitat provides food, water, shelter, and space. All living things, including people, share these same basic needs.

There are many different kinds of habitats. The climate, soil, and water determine what kinds of plants will grow in a habitat. Some habitats are dry and hot, like a desert. Other habitats are lush and green, like a forest. In each habitat, living things have adapted to the climate, soil, water, and other living things.

Living things in the same habitat depend on each other to survive. They are interdependent. Plants provide food and shelter for animals. Animals become food for other animals. All of the living things share the space in a habitat.

Various habitats can be found in your backyard, neighborhood, community, and region. Habitats can be very large and very small. Habitats are all around us—in cities, suburbs, and farming areas, as well as forests, meadows, deserts, rivers, and oceans. Investigate your own surroundings and discover the different habitats!

Name_____ Date_____

Habitats—Reading Comprehension Test

1 What is a habitat?

ⓐ a home for living things

ⓑ something you do again and again

ⓒ a type of plant

ⓓ an endangered species

2 True or False: All living things need food, water, shelter, and space to live.

ⓐ true

ⓑ false

3 To survive, living things in the same habitat depend on _____.

ⓐ rocks

ⓑ money

ⓒ trees

ⓓ each other

4 True or False: The climate, soil, and water determine what kinds of plants will grow in a habitat.

ⓐ true

ⓑ false

5 If you were in the desert, the habitat would probably be _____.

ⓐ lush and green

ⓑ wet and cold

ⓒ hot and dry

ⓓ cool and green

6 True or False: All habitats are very large.

ⓐ true

ⓑ false

Habitats © 2003 Creative Teaching Press

Language Arts

This Is a Habitat

OBJECTIVES

Students will
- identify the parts of a habitat.
- classify objects into living and nonliving things.

Display the Parts of a Habitat transparency. Explain that a habitat is the place where a plant or an animal lives. A habitat is made up of many living and nonliving parts. The living parts include plants and animals. The nonliving parts include rocks, soil, water, air, and temperature. These nonliving things determine the kinds of living things that can live in a particular habitat. Draw on the board a two-column chart labeled *Living* and *Nonliving.* Invite students to name things from the transparency that fit into each category. Record students' responses on the chart. Ask students to look for the living and nonliving things when they examine other habitats. Have students create a mobile that shows the living and nonliving things in a habitat. Give each student a wire hanger, construction paper, and string. Show students how to cover the open part of their hanger with construction paper and label it *Habitats.* Have students choose a specific habitat and then draw on separate paper shapes pictures of living and nonliving things in that habitat. Ask them to write a sentence on the back of each paper shape and use string to attach the shapes to their hanger. Ask them to hang the pictures of living things and nonliving things on separate ends of the hanger. Display the mobiles around the room. Invite students to read the information on each mobile.

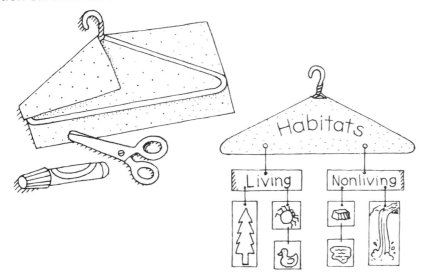

- Habitats mini-book (pages 24–26)
- Parts of a Habitat transparency
- scissors
- crayons or markers
- overhead projector

Habitat Mini-Book

OBJECTIVES

Students will
- identify and understand the parts of a habitat.
- identify a purpose for reading.

Copy a class set of the Habitats mini-book reproducibles. Give each student a set of mini-book pages. Ask students to cut apart their mini-book pages and place them in the correct order. Staple the left side of each student's pages to create a book. Invite students to color the pictures. Explain to the class that they will be using their book on numerous days for several activities. Explain that good readers have a purpose, or reason, for reading. Give some examples, such as to be entertained, to learn about someone, or to get information. Encourage students to read their mini-book to learn more about habitats. Divide the class into pairs. Ask pairs to take turns reading pages of the book. Bring the class together to review what they learned from their mini-book. Display the Parts of a Habitat transparency. Invite students to identify a feature on the transparency and compare it to one of the habitats in their mini-book. For example, a student might identify the large herbivore and note that in a grassland the large herbivore can be an antelope.

Habitats

A **habitat** is the place where a plant or an animal lives. A habitat has the space, water, shelter, and food that a living thing needs to survive. Living and nonliving things are found in a habitat. Five major habitats of Earth are the forest, grassland, desert, tundra, and aquatic environments.

Page 1

Defining Habitats

MATERIALS

● paper strips
● paper bag or box
● dictionaries
● large index cards

OBJECTIVES

Students will
● use a dictionary.
● determine syllables, parts of speech, and definitions of words.

List the following parts of speech on the board: *noun, verb, adjective, adverb.* Review examples for each part of speech. Then, have students practice counting the number of syllables in some words. Explain to students that a dictionary not only gives the definition of the word, but it also tells how many syllables a word has and the part of speech it is. Write the vocabulary words from page 8 on paper strips. Duplicate words as needed so each student will have a strip. Place the strips in a paper bag or box. Invite students to randomly select a strip. Divide the class into small groups. Give each group a dictionary and each student a large index card. Ask group members to assist one another as each student finds the following information for his or her word: part of speech, number of syllables, and the definition. Ask students to write their word in large letters on their index card and then neatly record the information about their word. Display all the word cards on a bulletin board. Use the cards to give clues for each vocabulary word. For example, *This word is a noun and has three syllables. It describes an animal that eats plants.* (herbivore) Invite volunteers to take turns giving clues.

biome

biome

a noun
2 syllables
a biome is habitats
around the world that
are similar

Habitat Mix-Up

OBJECTIVES

Students will
● use spelling patterns to unscramble words.
● match vocabulary words with their definitions.
● place words in alphabetical order.

Give each student a Habitat Mix-Up reproducible. Explain that the words on the left are from their mini-book. Ask students to unscramble each word. Then, have them draw a line that connects each word to its definition on the right. Review the answers with the class. Then, have students list the words in alphabetical order on the back of their paper. Students should answer 1. *plant, C;* 2. *shelter, D;* 3. *carnivore, A;* 4. *herbivore, E;* 5. *survive, B;* 6. *habitat, H;* 7. *permafrost, G;* 8. *temperature, F.*

Habitat Homonyms

OBJECTIVE

● Students will use context clues to identify homonyms.

Explain to students that homonyms are words that sound alike but have different spellings and meanings. Remind students that they should think about the meaning of a homonym to see if it works in a sentence. Give each student a Habitat Homonyms reproducible. As a class, read the definition for each homonym. Have students read each sentence and use the context clues to help them choose the correct homonym and circle it. Review the answers with the class.

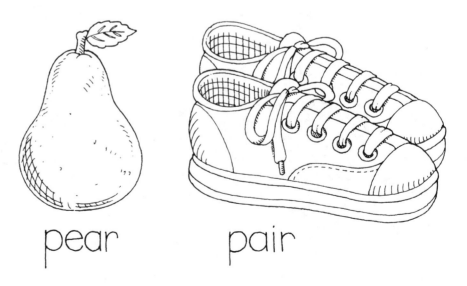

pear   pair

Habitat Information Posters

MATERIALS

- *What Is a Biome?* by Bobbie Kalman
- Habitat Information Organizer (page 29)
- completed Habitats mini-books (see page 14)
- poster board or butcher paper
- crayons or markers
- Internet and/or reference books

OBJECTIVES

Students will
- identify features of a habitat.
- use resource materials to find information.
- present information on a poster.
- make an oral presentation.

Explain that a biome is a very large area of similar habitats. Ask students to name the five habitats they read about in their mini-book, and list them on the board. Show students the cover of the book *What Is a Biome?* Invite students to make predictions about what they think they will learn in this book. After you read it to the class, brainstorm with students new information about habitats to add to the list on the board. Divide the class into small groups. Assign a habitat to each group, and give each group a Habitat Information Organizer. Ask groups to research facts about their habitat and write them on the organizer. Have groups use the information to design a poster that teaches others about the habitat. Brainstorm with students some of the information the poster should have (e.g., types of plants, sources of water, animals that live there, where on earth you would find that habitat). Invite groups to present their poster and explain the information on it to the class.

- World of an Animal reproducible (page 30)
- Internet and/or reference books
- chart paper
- crayons or markers

Animal Poetry

OBJECTIVES

Students will
- research an animal and its habitat.
- use information to write a patterned poem about an animal.

Give each student a World of an Animal reproducible. Have each student select an animal. Ask students to use books and the Internet to research the appearance, nature, habits, and habitat of their animal. Ask them to record this information on the reproducible. Explain that they will use this information to help them write a poem that follows a pattern. Write on chart paper the directions for the poem (shown below), and display it. Model the pattern of the poem's structure for the class. Ask students to write a poem and then illustrate it. Invite students to share their patterned poem with the class.

1 Write the name of an animal.

2 Write a two-word phrase that describes the animal.

3 Write a three-word phrase that describes an action the animal performs within its habitat.

4 Write a four-word phrase that describes the animal's habitat.

5 Write one word that describes or renames the animal.

Panda
Giant bear
Eating bamboo leaves
Living among the trees
Endangered

My Senses Tell Me

OBJECTIVES

Students will
- skim a text to look for information.
- describe a habitat using the five senses.
- write a descriptive paragraph.

MATERIALS

- chart paper
- completed Habitats mini-books (see page 14)
- reference books with pictures of habitats
- 9" x 12" (23 cm x 30.5 cm) construction paper
- scissors
- construction paper
- glue
- crayons or markers

In advance, write on chart paper the frame shown below. Have students skim their mini-book to review the types of habitats. Ask students to tell what they might see or hear as they name each type of habitat. List on the board the names of specific habitats such as a rain forest, a tidepool, or a meadow. Explain that our five senses are seeing, hearing, smelling, tasting, and touching. In each habitat, there are things that we can see, hear, smell, taste, and feel. Have each student choose one of the habitats from the list. Ask students to pretend they are observing the habitat and use their senses to describe it. Provide reference materials that show pictures of each habitat to help spark students' imaginations. Display the chart, and have students use the frame to organize their ideas. Then, help students form a topic sentence from the first line. Ask them to use each of the remaining sentences as a detail for the paragraph. Have students create a pop-up card to share their information. Demonstrate how to make a pop-up card following the pictures shown below. On the inside of the card, have students create a picture and label for their habitat. Then, ask students to write their completed paragraph on the back of the card. Display the completed pop-up cards around the room, and invite students to read them.

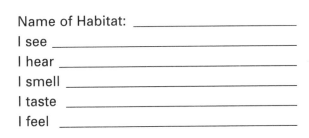

Name of Habitat: _____
I see _____
I hear _____
I smell _____
I taste _____
I feel _____

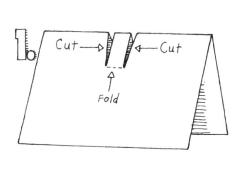

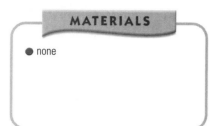

The Human Habitat

OBJECTIVES

Students will
● identify the parts of their own habitat.
● identify and write the four types of sentences.
● punctuate sentences correctly.

Remind students that they live in a habitat. Invite students to describe the habitat in which they live. Have them brainstorm the living and nonliving things that share their habitat space. Write students' ideas on the board. Then, ask students to use the ideas on the board to write each of the four types of sentences (question, statement, exclamation, and command). Write these examples on the board: *What do I find in my habitat? I share my habitat with other humans and my pets. I don't have to hunt for my food! Please keep my habitat clean.* Invite students to identify each sentence type from the examples. Review the purpose and punctuation of each sentence type. Have students write a statement, an exclamation, a question, and a command about their own habitat. Ask them to trade papers and check for correct punctuation. Invite volunteers to share their sentences with the class.

An Important Lesson

- *The Important Book* by Margaret Wise Brown
- An Important Paragraph reproducible (page 31)
- common objects (e.g., pencil, phone, food items)
- bookbinding materials

OBJECTIVES

Students will
- determine the main idea and supporting details in a passage.
- compose individual paragraphs.

Explain to students that everything is important for a reason. Show students several different objects and brainstorm why these things are important. Share *The Important Book* with students. Read aloud the first few pages from the book, and ask students if they notice a pattern. Then, lead a class discussion about the pattern frame *The important thing about _____ is _____.* Have students point out that each paragraph has the same beginning and ending, as well as details about the subject in between. Explain that the first sentence gives the main idea for the paragraph. The following sentences give details about the main idea. Then, the main idea is stated again at the end of the paragraph. Read aloud the remaining pages. Create a word bank by asking students to brainstorm the important features about each habitat. Give each student An Important Paragraph reproducible. Ask students to use the sentence frame to write a paragraph about the important features of a habitat. Have students use the paragraph editing checklist at the bottom of the page to review their completed paragraph and revise it as needed. Ask them to rewrite their revised paragraph on writing paper using neat handwriting. Create a class book by binding the papers together. Encourage students to read the class book.

The important thing
about a __rain forest__ is
it has __so many different__
__species__.

- Letter to a Friend reproducible (page 32)
- dictionaries

Letter to a Friend

OBJECTIVES

Students will
- identify the parts of a friendly letter.
- edit a letter.
- correct misspelled words.

Discuss with students the parts of a friendly letter. Model how a friendly letter is dated, begins with a greeting, and ends with a closing and a signature. Remind students that the body of the letter follows the same rules as any paragraph: first line is indented, sentences are complete, and sentences begin with a capital letter and have ending punctuation. Give each student a Letter to a Friend reproducible. Invite students to identify what is wrong with this letter (the date, greeting, closing, and signature are missing). Explain to students that they will use their own name for the signature and they will need to date the letter and choose a friend who will "receive" it. Divide the class into small groups. Tell students that each sentence in the letter has one misspelled word. Remind students to check words in a dictionary if they are unsure of the spelling. Explain to students that each sentence is missing its ending punctuation. Ask groups to work together to find the mistakes. Then, each student should add a date, greeting, and closing to his or her own letter. Review with the class the correct spelling of words and the proper punctuation that ends each sentence.

Letter to a Friend

Directions: Parts of this letter are missing. Add the missing parts. Add the correct punctuation to the end of each sentence. Circle and correct one misspelled word in each sentence.

January 19

Dear Joey,

Do you know much about a habbitatt called the tundra The tundra is a cold, drie part of the world It is found cloze to the Arctic Circle The tundra is also fownd at the top of high mountains There are very few planttes and animals that live there Tundra forms becuz of the climate The winters are long and coldd Plants do not have a long tyme to grow There is a layer of soil calld the permafrost Wow, the permafrost never thaws owt

Do any aminals live in the tundra In the sumer, mountain goats, caribou, snow leopards, and llamas are found in the tundra Gee, I would onely want to visit the tundra in the summer What doo you think

Sincerely,

Teresa

Habitat ABCs

- recommended alphabet books (see below)
- construction paper
- crayons and markers

OBJECTIVE

- Students will work cooperatively to create a habitat alphabet book.

Share examples of alphabet books, and point out that authors usually have a theme for these books. The words used in an alphabet book support that theme. Have students work together to create an alphabet book about habitats. Make a list of the letters of the alphabet on the board. Call out a letter of the alphabet, and invite volunteers to say a word that begins with the letter and is related to habitats (e.g., D is for desert). Write the word on the board after the letter. Then, ask students to brainstorm a sentence that tells about the word (e.g., Deserts can be hot and sandy, but they can also be cold). Brainstorm words for every letter of the alphabet. For difficult letters like X and Y, adjust the rules by telling students they can use a word that contains that letter instead. Then, assign one to two letters to each student. Have students write the letter and word at the top of a construction paper page and a sentence at the bottom of the page. Ask them to illustrate their letter/sentence in the open space on the page. Combine the pages to create a class alphabet book titled *Habitats from A to Z.* Encourage students to read the class book.

- *Alphabet City* by Steven T. Johnson (The Penguin Group)
- *Apples, Bubbles, and Crystals: Your Science ABCs* by Andrea T. Bennett and James H. Kessler (McGraw-Hill)
- *G Is for Google: A Math Alphabet Book* by David Schwartz (Ten Speed Press)
- *Jambo Means Hello* by Muriel L. Feelings (Puffin Pied Piper)

Habitats

Habitats

A **habitat** is the place where a plant or an animal lives. A habitat has the space, water, shelter, and food that a living thing needs to survive. Living and nonliving things are found in a habitat. Five major habitats of Earth are the forest, grassland, desert, tundra, and aquatic environments.

Page 1

The **aquatic** habitat is the largest on Earth. Many plants and animals call the water their home. The aquatic habitat can be divided into **freshwater** or **marine water.** Freshwater habitats include ponds, rivers, lakes, and wetlands. Marine water habitats include oceans, tidepools, **estuaries,** and coral reefs.

Page 2

Habitats

The **forest** habitat is the second largest on Earth. **Tropical forests** are near the equator. All tropical forests receive a large amount of rainfall. Many different kinds of plants and animals live in the tropical forest. **Temperate forests** have cold, wet winters and warm summers. Evergreen and **deciduous** trees are found in temperate forests. **Boreal forests** are found in very cold areas. Most of the trees are **conifers**. The summers are short and the winters are long, cold, and dry.

Page 3

The **desert** habitats of Earth are harsh places to live. Deserts get less than 20 inches (50 cm) of rain a year. The plants and animals that live in a desert habitat need to be able to store water and withstand the heat. Very few tall plants and large animals live in the desert because they cannot store enough water. Many animals in the desert are **nocturnal** because the temperature is cooler at night.

Page 4

Habitats

The **tundra** is the coldest of all habitats. There is very little rain or snow. The winter is so long, plants have very little time to grow. Animals use the fat on their bodies to protect them from the cold. The tundra of the arctic has a layer of soil called the **permafrost**. The permafrost is always frozen.

Page 5

The **grassland** habitat has grasses instead of many shrubs or trees. Grasslands have hot, dry summers and short rainy seasons. Many large herbivores live in this habitat. These **herbivores** travel in herds and are hunted by **carnivores**. The savanna, plains, steppe, veldt, and prairies are all examples of grasslands.

Page 6

Habitat Mix-Up

Directions: Unscramble the vocabulary words and write each word on the line. Then, draw a line to connect the word to its definition.

1 tapln

_____

2 reshlet

_____

3 arncireov

_____

4 erirehbov

_____

5 usviver

_____

6 tabahit

_____

7 storefmarp

_____

8 peramettrue

_____

A an animal that only eats other animals

B to stay alive

C the beginning of all food chains

D a place that protects or covers

E an animal that only eats plants

F the hotness or coldness of a place

G a layer of soil that is always frozen

H the home of a plant or an animal

Habitat Homonyms

Directions: Read the definitions for each pair of homonyms. Read each sentence. Use the context of the sentence to help you choose the correct homonym.

there: at or in that place their: belonging to them	two: a number, 2 too: also
know: to understand no: not so	pear: a fruit pair: a set of 2
eight: a number, 8 ate: past tense for "eat"	sea: a body of salt water see: to take in with the eyes

1 Sea turtles eat soft foods. They use (their, there) sharp, horny jaws to shred food.

2 Sea otters (no, know) how to crack shells open on rocks.

3 A starfish pried open a clamshell and (eight, ate) the meat inside.

4 Many birds live along the seashore (too, two).

5 A (pear, pair) of sandpipers poke into the sand with their long beaks.

6 You can (see, sea) fat seals sunning themselves on the rocky shore.

pear

pair

Habitats © 2003 Creative Teaching Press

Habitat Information Organizer

The name of the habitat I will research is

Where in the world is this habitat?

These are some of the nonliving things in the habitat:

This is the climate of the habitat:

These animals are found in the habitat:

These plants are found in the habitat:

Here are other special facts about the habitat:

World of an Animal

Name of animal: _____

Draw a picture of the animal.

Is the animal an herbivore, a carnivore, or an omnivore?

_____

Is the animal a mammal, a bird, a fish, a reptile, or an amphibian?

_____

Describe how the animal looks._____

_____

_____

In what habitat is the animal found? _____

What is the animal's habitat? (where and when it sleeps, what it eats, who its enemies are)

_____

_____

Why is this animal important to its ecosystem? Why should it be protected?_____

_____

Habitats © 2003 Creative Teaching Press

Name_____ Date_____

An Important Paragraph

The important thing about _____ is _____.

_____

_____

_____

_____

_____

_____

_____

_____

_____

_____

Use the checklist to proofread your paragraph.

☐ I indented the first line of my paragraph.

☐ Each sentence is a complete thought.

☐ Each sentence starts with a capital letter.

☐ Each sentence ends with the correct punctuation.

☐ I checked the spelling of difficult words in a dictionary.

☐ I rewrote my paragraph on clean writing paper in my best handwriting.

Staple your revised paragraph on top of this page.

Letter to a Friend

Directions: Parts of this letter are missing. Add the missing parts. Add the correct punctuation to the end of each sentence. Circle and correct one misspelled word in each sentence.

_____

_____

Do you know much about a habbitatt called the tundra The tundra is a cold, drie part of the world   It is found cloze to the Arctic Circle The tundra is also fownd at the top of high mountains   There are very few planttes and animals that live there Tundra forms becuz of the climate   The winters are long and coldd   Plants do not have a long tyme to grow There is a layer of soil calld the permafrost Wow, the permafrost never thaws owt

Do any aminals live in the tundra   In the sumer, mountain goats, caribou, snow leopards, and llamas are found in the tundra Gee, I would onely want to visit the tundra in the summer What doo you think

_____

_____

Math

Savanna Math

OBJECTIVES

Students will
- use concrete objects to tell story problems.
- write and solve addition and subtraction equations.

MATERIALS

- Savanna Math reproducible (page 39)
- Savanna Animals reproducible (page 40)
- scissors

Explain to students that the savanna is a part of the grassland habitat. The savanna is found in Africa. Divide the class into small groups. Give each group a Savanna Math and a Savanna Animals reproducible. Have students describe the plants and nonliving parts shown in the habitat. Ask groups to cut apart the animal pictures. Invite students to identify some of the animals on the second reproducible. Have one student in each group begin by telling an addition or subtraction story problem using the animal pictures and the drawing of the savanna. For example, *There were three lions resting in the shade. (Student places three lion pictures under the tree.) Two lions walked away. (Student removes two of the pictures.)* The other members of the group write an equation for the problem on a piece of writing paper. After the group agrees on the equation, ask students to solve it. Have group members compare their answers. Ask group members to take turns telling addition or subtraction story problems.

Savanna Math

3 − 2 = 1

- Animal Patterns reproducible (page 41)
- plastic chips in assorted colors
- crayons or markers

Patterns of the Desert

OBJECTIVES

Students will
- identify animals and plants of the desert habitat.
- identify a pattern.
- create a symbolic representation of a pattern.

Give each student an Animal Patterns reproducible. Ask students to identify some of the plants and animals on the reproducible. Divide the class into pairs. Give each pair some plastic chips. Explain that in each row, the living things form a pattern. Ask pairs to choose a color chip to represent each different animal in one row. Have them match up the chips to each different animal in the same order. Ask them to identify the pattern the chip colors make and color in the pattern on the reproducible. Then, ask them to continue the pattern by drawing in the animals and coloring in the chips. Invite volunteers to share the patterns they identified with the class. To extend the lesson, have students use their patterns to create word problems. For example, *If there are six roadrunners and three scorpions, how many more roadrunners are there?*

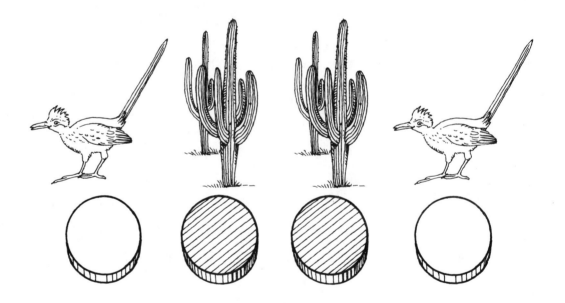

Kelp Forest Graphing

OBJECTIVES

Students will
- collect and record data.
- create a bar graph.
- interpret information from a bar graph.

MATERIALS

- Kelp Forest Creature Cards (page 42)
- Kelp Forest Graphing reproducible (page 43)
- card stock
- scissors
- paper bags
- crayons or markers

In advance, make several copies of the Kelp Forest Creature Cards on card stock. Cut apart the creature cards, and mix them up. Make a "kelp forest bag" for each small group of students by dropping a random quantity of the cards into a paper bag. Explain to students that the kelp forest is a habitat under the sea. The kelp provides food and shelter for many animals. Divide the class into small groups, and give each group a kelp forest bag. Give each student a Kelp Forest Graphing reproducible. Have groups "study" the animals in their kelp forest bag by emptying it and sorting the cards. Then, ask groups to create and color a bar graph on the reproducible. Remind them to title their graph. Ask students to answer the questions using their completed bar graph.

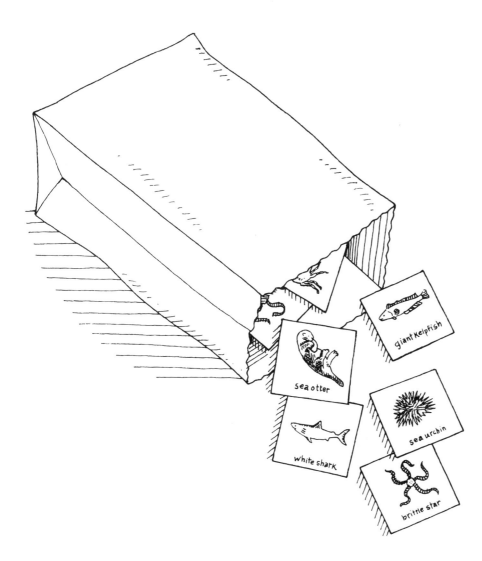

Early Bird Gets the Worm

MATERIALS

- Catching Worms reproducible (page 44)
- small paper bags
- ½" by 4" (13 mm by 10 cm) green, brown, red, and blue paper strips
- spring-type clothespins
- colored markers that match the colors of the paper strips

OBJECTIVES

Students will
- understand that a consumer is an animal that eats other animals or plants.
- understand that camouflage helps protect animals.
- collect data.
- complete a bar graph.

In advance, write each student's name on a paper bag. Explain to the class that in a habitat, a consumer is an animal that eats other animals or plants. Explain to students that birds are considered consumers and that they are going to pretend to be birds. Discuss what birds eat. Take the class to a grassy area outside. Show students the paper strips, and explain that these are "worms." Sprinkle the worms over a large area. Explain to students that they are going to be birds searching for worms. Pass out the paper sacks. Give each student a clothespin, and explain that it will be their "beak." Demonstrate how to use the clothespin to pick up a worm. Tell students they will have to operate the beak with one hand and keep the other hand behind their back at all times. The paper bag is their "nest." As they collect worms, they run back to the nest and place the worms in the bag. Divide the class into small groups. Position each group around the perimeter of the area. Allow only one group to "go catch worms" at a time, limiting each group's time in the area to 30 seconds. After each group has had a turn, have students fold over the top of their bag to close it, and help you clean up the remaining strips. Return to the classroom. Ask groups to record the names of each group member and the number of strips each member found on the Catching Worms reproducible. Have them color each box to match the color of the strip and then use the completed bar graph to answer the questions at the bottom of the page. Discuss the results with the class. Ask students *Which "worms" were easiest to find? Which was the hardest to find? Why do you think this was so?*

Rain Forest Problem Solving

MATERIALS

● Rain Forest Problem Solving
reproducible (page 45)

OBJECTIVES

Students will
● solve story problems.
● identify extra information in a story problem.
● learn about plants and animals of the tropical rain forest.

Explain to the class that a tropical rain forest gets more than 80 inches (203 cm) of rain a year. The temperature is usually around 70°F to 85°F (21°C to 29°C) at any given time. Because of these moist, hot conditions, many different types of plants grow in the rain forest. The abundance of plants can support many different kinds of animals. Although rain forests cover less than 7 percent of the earth's land surface, scientists think that over 50 percent of all the kinds of living things in the world live in this place. Give each student a Rain Forest Problem Solving reproducible. Explain that the reproducible presents some information about some of the plants and animals of the tropical rain forest. They will also solve math problems, but each problem includes some information they do not need to solve the problem. Read the first problem together. Ask *What are we asked to find out?* (how many capybaras there were in all) *What information do we need to solve the problem?* (the number of capybaras eating grass and how many joined them) *What information is extra and not needed to solve the problem?* (Capybaras are the largest rodents in the world.) Have students draw a line through the extra information. Divide the class into pairs. Have pairs work together to solve the problems. Invite pairs to share their answers with the class. Students should answer 1. *28 capybaras,* 2. *22 inches (56 cm),* 3. *8 okapis,* 4. *20 flies,* 5. *13 frogs.*

Habitat Hog

- Habitat Hog reproducible (page 46)
- crayons or markers
- dice

OBJECTIVES

Students will
- use manipulatives to solve addition problems.
- add three numbers.
- record problems in pictorial and symbolic form.

Explain to the class that space is an important part of a plant or an animal's habitat. Have students play Habitat Hog to compete for space in a "habitat." Divide the class into pairs. Give each pair a Habitat Hog reproducible, crayons or markers, and two dice. Explain that the reproducible is their habitat and they will compete for the available space. The object of the game is to take up more of the space (squares) in the habitat than your partner. Ask partners to choose different-colored markers. The first partner rolls the dice, uses the two numbers to write an addition problem, and colors in the total number of squares. The partner repeats this action. Then, the first player takes another turn, but this time, he or she adds the previous sum to the new sum. In this manner, each player keeps a running sum of the total number of squares each has colored. Encourage partners to color squares that are connected at first, but when the board is mostly filled, they can color squares where they can find blank ones. When players have colored in all the squares, have players count their squares. The player with the highest sum, and therefore the most squares, wins.

Savanna Math

Savanna Animals

Habitats © 2003 Creative Teaching Press

Animal Patterns

Directions: Choose a color chip to represent the different animals in a row. Match chips to animals to make a pattern. Color in the chips to match the pattern. Continue the animal and chip pattern.

Kelp Forest Creature Cards

white shark	kelp crab	giant kelpfish	sea otter
white shark	kelp crab	giant kelpfish	sea otter
white shark	kelp crab	giant kelpfish	sea otter
sea urchin	brittle star	brittle star	brittle star
sea urchin	sea urchin	sea urchin	brittle star

Habitats © 2003 Creative Teaching Press

Name_____ Date_____

Kelp Forest Graphing

Directions: Fill out the bar graph. Color each square to match an animal in your kelp forest. Answer the questions.

Title: _____

Name of Animals

	1	2	3	4	5	6	7	8
white shark								
kelp crab								
giant kelpfish								
sea otter								
sea urchin								
brittle star								

Number of Animals

Which animal had the highest number? _____

Which animal had the lowest number? _____

What was the difference between the highest and lowest number? _____

How many different animals were in your kelp forest? _____

Was there the same amount of any animals? _____ What were they? _____

_____

Write a math problem to be solved using your graph. Have a classmate solve it.

_____

_____

Answer: _____ Solved by _____

Catching Worms

Directions: Write the name of each person in your group. Record the number of colored worms each person collected. Color each square to match the worm color. Title your graph. Answer the questions.

Name of Student

1   2   3   4   5   6   7   8   9   10

Number of Worms

Which color worm was collected the most? _____

Which color worm was collected the least? _____

Why do you think this happened? _____

Who collected the most worms in your group? _____

Who collected the fewest worms? _____

Write a story problem that uses the information from your graph.

_____

_____

_____

Name_____ Date_____

Rain Forest Problem Solving

Directions: Read each problem. Draw a line through the information you do not need to solve the problem. Then, solve the problem.

1 Capybaras are the largest rodents in the world. 16 capybaras were eating grasses by the river. 12 more capybaras joined them. How many capybaras were there in all?

_____

2 The rafflesia flower is 24 inches (61 cm) wide. It has a very stinky smell like rotten meat. The rosy periwinkle flower is only 2 inches (5 cm) wide. How much wider is the rafflesia flower?

_____

3 14 okapis drank water from the river. 6 okapis wandered off. Okapis can clean their ears with their long tongues. How many okapis were left at the river?

_____

4 A leaf-tailed gecko caught and ate 11 flies. Leaf-tailed geckos have unusual leaf-shaped tails. The gecko later caught and ate 9 more flies. How many flies did the gecko eat?

_____

5 Flying frogs use their large, webbed feet like a parachute. 21 flying frogs live in a tree. 8 of the flying frogs glided to the ground. How many frogs were left in the tree?

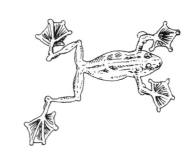

_____

Names of Players_____   Date_____

Habitat Hog

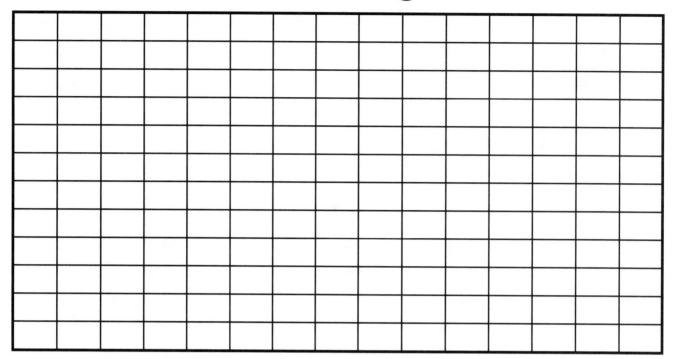

Player 1: _____   Player 2: _____

_____ + _____ = _____ Total Sum

_____ + _____ = _____

_____ + _____ = _____

_____ + _____ = _____

_____ + _____ = _____

_____ + _____ = _____

_____ + _____ = _____

_____ + _____ = _____

_____ + _____ = _____

_____ + _____ = _____

_____ + _____ = _____ Total Sum

_____ + _____ = _____

_____ + _____ = _____

_____ + _____ = _____

_____ + _____ = _____

_____ + _____ = _____

_____ + _____ = _____

_____ + _____ = _____

_____ + _____ = _____

Habitats © 2003 Creative Teaching Press

Science

Creating a Habitat

MATERIALS

- World of an Animal reproducible (page 30)
- index cards
- Internet and/or reference materials
- shoe boxes
- assorted craft supplies (e.g., glue, scissors, construction paper, twigs and leaves, fabric, craft sticks, crayons or markers)

OBJECTIVES

Students will
- learn about the major components of a habitat.
- understand the specific needs of a species.
- design an artificial habitat that meets the needs of a species.

In advance, write the names of the following animals on index cards: *penguin, komodo dragon, kangaroo rat, toucan, anteater, scarab beetle,* and *sea urchin.* Explain to the class that they will pretend to have a job at the zoo. Brainstorm with the class a list of ten things an animal may need to have in its habitat to survive. Then, have the class pick the four most important things the animal could not do without. Their list should include food, water, shelter, and adequate space. Remind the class that these are the things provided by a natural habitat. To keep an animal healthy and happy, a zoo should try to copy the animal's natural habitat as closely as possible. Divide the class into seven groups. Give each group one of the index cards. Ask groups to create a zoo habitat that meets the needs of their animal. Give each group a World of an Animal reproducible, and ask groups to use books or the Internet to research information about the animal's natural habitat. Then, have groups use this information, a shoe box, and craft supplies to create a diorama that shows the animal's zoo habitat. Invite groups to share and explain their diorama with the class.

- Chain Game reproducible (page 51)
- card stock
- scissors

The Food Chain Connection

OBJECTIVES

Students will
- learn that the living things in a habitat form a food chain.
- learn that plants are the beginning of a food chain.
- organize plants and animals from a single habitat into a food chain.

Copy the Chain Game reproducible onto card stock for each student. Explain to students that living things need food to give them energy. Energy moves through a food chain. A food chain is the path by which energy passes from one living thing to another. Green plants are the beginning of all food chains. Green plants are called producers because they produce food for animals to eat. Animals are called consumers because they consume other living things for food. Consumers that only eat plants are called herbivores. Consumers that eat only meat are called carnivores. Some animals eat plants and other animals and are called omnivores. Give each student a Chain Game reproducible. Have students cut apart the cards. Ask them to name the animals on the cards and explain which ones form a food chain. Then, divide the class into small groups to play the Chain Game. The object of the game is to collect the three cards that make a food chain in a habitat. Have each player contribute his or her set of nine cards to make a deck of cards. Ask one student to deal seven cards and then place the rest of the cards facedown in a pile. The first player asks the person on the right if he or she has a particular card. For example, *Do you have a carnivore from the desert?* If the answer is "yes," the card trades hands. If the answer is "no," the player selects a card from the pile. Whenever players have a food chain set, they lay the set out in front of them in the correct food chain order. Play continues around the circle until students have placed all cards in sets. The player with the most sets wins.

Desert Plant

Desert Herbivore

Desert Carnivore

Animals in Danger

OBJECTIVE

● Students will learn about endangered and/or extinct animals.

MATERIALS

● Animals in Danger reproducible (page 52)

● dictionaries

● encyclopedias and/or Internet

Explain to students that many living things become endangered as human populations continue to grow. Plants and animals lose their habitat when it is changed into houses, cities, and roads. In addition, some animals are hunted for their fur, feathers, horns, or tusks. When a population of living things is in immediate danger of extinction, we say they are endangered. A population of living things is extinct when it is no longer living anywhere on Earth. Give each student an Animals in Danger reproducible. Divide the class into small groups. Give each group a dictionary and access to an encyclopedia. Assign each group two or three animals from the list on the reproducible. Have groups research their animals and determine if each animal is extinct or endangered. Bring groups together to share their findings. Then, have them search for the remaining endangered animals in the word search puzzle. Ask groups to share their completed puzzle with the class. These animals are extinct and are not in the puzzle: *dodo, passenger pigeon, great auk, Carolina parakeet, quagga, moa.*

Endangered Animal Education

OBJECTIVES

Students will
● educate others about endangered animals.
● design a persuasive poster.

MATERIALS

● Animals in Danger reproducible (page 52)

● research books and/or Internet

● construction paper

● crayons or markers

Divide the class into pairs. Give each pair the name of an endangered animal from the Animals in Danger reproducible. Remember that six animals from the reproducible are extinct (see Animals in Danger, above). Have pairs research the animal to learn why it is endangered and what can be done to protect it. Ask pairs to design a poster that persuades other people to learn about and help protect the endangered animal. Invite pairs to share their completed poster with the class.

● Ecosystem Observation reproducible (page 53)

● string cut into 12¼' (3.73 m) lengths

● clipboards

Square-Yard Ecosystems

OBJECTIVES

Students will
● make observations of a ecosystem.
● be able to describe how living things work together in an ecosystem.

In advance, tie each length of string to make a loop. Explain to students that an ecologist is a scientist who studies ecosystems. Ecologists use the term *ecosystem* to describe how living and non-living things work together in a habitat. Ecologists study the different kinds of living things in an ecosystem. They watch how the living things interact with each other and the nonliving part of the ecosystem. Explain to students that they will become ecologists and study a square-yard ecosystem. Give each student an Ecosystem Observation reproducible and a clipboard. Divide the class into small groups. Give each group a loop of string. Bring groups outside to an area with minimal foot traffic. Ask groups to lay their string in a square on the ground to form a boundary of an ecosystem. Then, ask groups to carefully observe the living things that are present in this ecosystem. Have them record their observations on their reproducible. Have groups also note any organisms that come into and leave the boundary of the square yard. Challenge groups to note how any of the living things interact with nonliving things or each other. Repeat observations over several days. Discuss the findings of each group with the class.

Chain Game

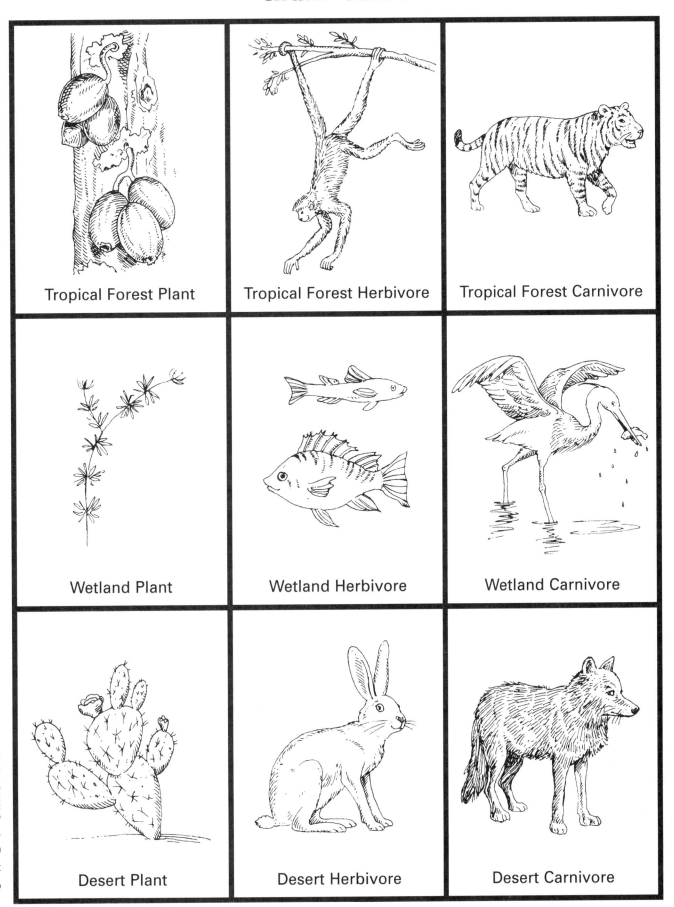

Tropical Forest Plant

Tropical Forest Herbivore

Tropical Forest Carnivore

Wetland Plant

Wetland Herbivore

Wetland Carnivore

Desert Plant

Desert Herbivore

Desert Carnivore

Animals in Danger

Directions: Circle the six animals that are extinct. Find and circle the remaining endangered animals in the puzzle below.

dodo	spotted owl	passenger pigeon	quagga	great auk
bontebok	Grevy's zebra	black rhinoceros	crocodile	manatee
indri	Arabian oryx	brown hyena	bald eagle	gorilla
moa	indigo macaw	Carolina parakeet	kakapo	cheetah

b	p	b	r	o	w	n	h	y	e	n	a	c	d	i
o	l	p	f	t	h	i	d	i	o	p	w	a	a	n
n	d	a	r	a	b	i	a	n	o	r	y	x	m	d
t	q	w	c	e	t	r	y	u	i	o	p	l	a	i
e	j	h	g	k	f	d	s	a	k	j	g	k	n	g
b	k	l	g	o	r	i	l	l	a	z	r	x	a	o
o	c	v	b	n	m	h	r	g	k	b	e	t	t	m
k	h	m	y	j	k	u	i	a	a	e	v	s	e	a
t	i	n	d	r	i	w	a	n	p	e	y	s	e	c
r	e	a	w	e	o	p	q	g	o	g	s	g	o	a
u	j	r	d	c	y	w	s	o	g	c	z	d	m	w
c	r	o	c	o	d	i	l	e	y	u	e	i	e	s
y	e	d	k	r	w	q	b	u	p	d	b	r	c	m
k	t	c	h	e	e	t	a	h	y	w	r	h	o	p
a	a	a	r	u	l	e	w	x	y	z	a	r	g	s
s	p	o	t	t	e	d	o	w	l	f	t	i	i	o
d	g	h	o	b	a	l	d	e	a	g	l	e	w	p

Name_____ Date_____

Ecosystem Observation

Where my ecosystem is found:

Living things I see in my ecosystem:	Nonliving things I see in my ecosystem:

How did the living things interact with the nonliving things?

How did the living things interact with each other?

Did any living or nonliving things cross over the boundary of the ecosystem? If so, what were they?

How did the ecosystem change over time?

Social Studies

- Map of a Wetland reproducible (page 59)

- overhead projector/transparency

A Map of a Wetland

OBJECTIVES

Students will
- use coordinates to find locations on a map.
- give coordinates for a specific location.
- use a map key.

In advance, copy the Map of a Wetland reproducible onto an overhead transparency. Explain to students that a map can show the features of a habitat. Any location on a map can be found by using a set of coordinates. The coordinates on a map is a pair made up of a letter and a number. Display the transparency. Have students locate the letters down the left side of the map and the numbers across the top. Explain that you would like them to find what is located at (B, 6). Model with the transparency how to find B on the left side and 6 at the top. Trace your fingers down and over until they meet in one box. Ask a volunteer to identify the symbol in (B, 6). Then, demonstrate how to give the coordinates of another symbol on the map. Tell students that you want to find the location of the reeds. Point out the symbol on the key that stands for reeds. Then, point to the reeds on the map. Demonstrate how to follow the row to the left and the column up to find the coordinates (D, 3). Give each student a Map of a Wetland reproducible. Divide the class into pairs. Have pairs work together to answer the questions at the bottom of the reproducible. Review the answers with the class.

The **aquatic** habitat is the largest on Earth. Many plants and animals call the water their home. The aquatic habitat can be divided into **freshwater** or **marine water.** Freshwater habitats include ponds, rivers, lakes, and wetlands. Marine water habitats include oceans, tidepools, **estuaries,** and coral reefs.

Page 2

Where in the World?

OBJECTIVES

Students will
- find locations of countries and continents on a world map.
- place endangered animals in the correct place on a world map.

MATERIALS

- World Map reproducible (page 60)
- chart paper
- Internet and/or resources about endangered species
- paper grocery bags
- scissors
- crayons or markers

In advance, list the names of endangered animals on chart paper. (See the examples shown below.) Display the list. Give each student a World Map reproducible. Have students work individually or in small groups. Give them access to research materials about endangered animals. Ask students to write the name of each animal from the list in the correct place on their world map. Then, ask them to choose one of the animals and design an "endangered species vest" to inform others about this animal. Give each student a paper grocery bag. Demonstrate how to press the opened bag flat, cut armholes and a neckhole, and cut the bag up the front to make a vest. Then, ask students to write information about their animal on the vest. Encourage students to add illustrations to the vest.

American black bear	peregrine falcon	Asian elephant
gorilla	red kangaroo	lemur
leopard	margay	ocelot
orangutan	panda	Galapagos penguin
black rhinoceros	tiger	humpback whale
wallaby	manatee	

● Geography of a Forest reproducible (page 61)

Geography of a Forest

OBJECTIVES

Students will
● plot locations on a map.
● use a map key.

Remind students that a map can show the features of a habitat. Explain to students that coordinates can be used to place landmarks and features of a habitat on a map. Ask students to pretend they are exploring a forest habitat. Give each student a Geography of a Forest reproducible. Have students identify and read the map key. Demonstrate how to use the coordinates to find a location. Divide the class into pairs, or have students work independently. Ask students to follow the directions to place on the map each feature of the forest. Review the completed maps with the class.

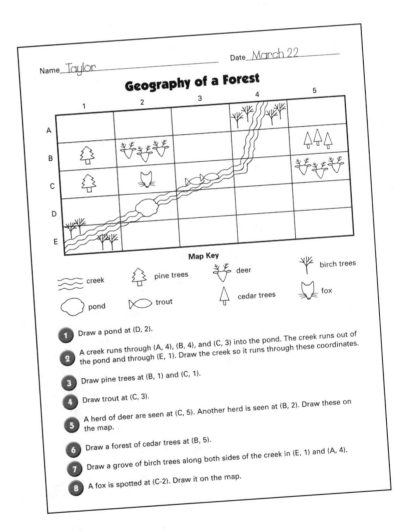

A Trip to the Arctic

MATERIALS

- Internet and/or books about the Arctic
- 6" x 9" (15 cm x 23 cm) construction paper
- 8½" x 5½" (22 cm x 14 cm) white paper
- crayons or markers

OBJECTIVES

Students will
- describe details of a particular habitat.
- work as a group to determine what is seen or done on a trip to a habitat location.

Explain to students that they will pretend they are taking a trip to the Arctic. Divide the class into small groups. Ask groups to list features of the Arctic. List on the board some of the information they should research: the climate, geography, seasons, places to see, plants and animals that live there, events to attend, or places to stay. Have groups research the Arctic to find out additional facts about this habitat. Finally, after all research is complete, have groups come to a consensus on whether or not they would recommend a trip to the Arctic. Remind students that they need to give reasons why they would or would not recommend a trip there. Then, ask students to use their research to make a "passport." Give each student construction paper for a cover and two sheets of white paper. Demonstrate how to make a passport. Have students record in their passport information they have researched about a trip to the Arctic. Have them illustrate their passport. Invite students to share their completed passport with the class.

- *A House is a House for Me* by Mary Ann Hoberman

- 8½" x 11" (21.5 cm x 28 cm) unlined paper

- crayons or markers

A Home for Me

OBJECTIVES

Students will
- identify the elements of a habitat.
- identify the favorite elements of their own habitat.
- write a descriptive paragraph.

Read to the class *A House is a House for Me.* Remind students of the elements of a habitat: food, water, shelter, and space. Have students brainstorm a list of their favorites for each element (e.g., food: pizza, apples, cheeseburgers; water: lakes, streams, ocean). Then, ask each student to list on a piece of paper his or her favorite choice for each element. Have students use this list to create a step book that illustrates their favorite elements of their ideal habitat. Give each student three sheets of paper, and demonstrate how to overlap the sheets, leaving a 1-inch (2.5-cm) margin at the bottom of each page. Have students hold the pages firmly as they fold over the top. The book now has six pages. Assist any students who are having difficulty. Staple each student's book through all layers next to the fold. Have students write a title on the cover page. Then, ask them to write a sentence on the bottom margin of each page. Have them draw an illustration for each page. Invite students to take turns reading each other's completed step books.

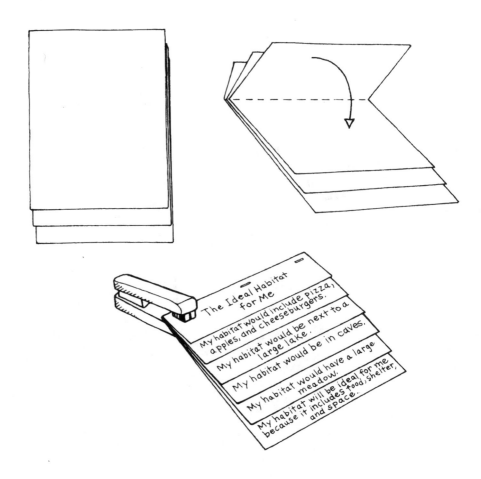

Map of a Wetland

	1	2	3	4	5	6
A		river		high ground		bird colony
B		river				mangrove trees
C		river				
D	river		reeds			
E	high ground		bird colony		crocodile nest	mangrove trees
F	high ground				mangrove trees	mangrove trees

Map Key

 reeds   bird colony   mangrove trees

 river   crocodile nest   high ground

1 What is located at (A, 6)? _____

2 What is the location of the crocodile nest?_____

3 What would you find at (E, 3)? _____

4 Mangrove trees grow at (F, 6). Give one more place where they grow._____

5 What is located at (D, 3)? _____

6 Where is the river located? Give all the coordinates. _____

World Map

Name_____ Date_____

Geography of a Forest

	1	2	3	4	5
A					
B					
C					
D					
E					

Map Key

 creek   pine trees   deer   birch trees

 pond    trout   cedar trees   fox

1 Draw a pond at (D, 2).

2 A creek runs through (A, 4), (B, 4), and (C, 3) into the pond. The creek runs out of the pond and through (E, 1). Draw the creek so it runs through these coordinates.

3 Draw pine trees at (B, 1) and (C, 1).

4 Draw trout at (C, 3).

5 A herd of deer are seen at (C, 5). Another herd is seen at (B, 2). Draw these on the map.

6 Draw a forest of cedar trees at (B, 5).

7 Draw a grove of birch trees along both sides of the creek in (E, 1) and (A, 4).

8 A fox is spotted at (C-2). Draw it on the map.

Habitats © 2003 Creative Teaching Press

Name_____ Date_____

Habitats Cumulative Test

Directions: Fill in the best answer for each question.

1 A friendly letter should include

_____.

ⓐ a greeting

ⓑ a math problem

ⓒ a stamp

ⓓ a book

2 A habitat is _____.

ⓐ something you do over and over

ⓑ a funny noise

ⓒ the natural home of a plant or an animal

ⓓ the space around a plant

3 Which sentence uses the underlined homonym correctly?

ⓐ I saw a <u>pear</u> of turtles by the pond.

ⓑ The grasshopper <u>eight</u> the leaves from the shrub.

ⓒ The <u>see</u> is home to many kinds of fish.

ⓓ There are <u>no</u> more passenger pigeons in the world.

4 Which list of habitats is in alphabetical order?

ⓐ desert, ocean, mountains, rain forest, tundra

ⓑ desert, mountains, ocean, rain forest, tundra

ⓒ desert, mountains, ocean, tundra, rain forest

ⓓ ocean, desert, mountains, rain forest, tundra

beavers										
ducks										
frogs										
trout										
	1	2	3	4	5	6	7	8	9	10

5 Look at the bar graph. How many more frogs than trout were found in the pond?

ⓐ 4

ⓑ 2

ⓒ 1

ⓓ 3

6 Look at the bar graph. Altogether, how many animals were found in the pond?

ⓐ 20

ⓑ 12

ⓒ 8

ⓓ 24

Habitats Cumulative Test

7 Which of these sentences is **not** written correctly?

ⓐ The desert can be a cold dry place?

ⓑ How many beetles do you see?

ⓒ I've never seen this many flowers before!

ⓓ The rain forest gets a lot of rain.

8 An animal that eats only plants is called _____.

ⓐ a producer

ⓑ an herbivore

ⓒ an omnivore

ⓓ a carnivore

9 Extinction is _____.

ⓐ when a population is in danger

ⓑ a smelly location

ⓒ when a population of plants or animals disappears

ⓓ the name of a habitat

10 Mule deer are herbivores. At the edge of the forest, 11 mule deer were grazing. 7 of the mule deer were adults. How many of the mule deer were **not** adults?

ⓐ 18

ⓑ 7

ⓒ 4

ⓓ 3

11 Name two nonliving things in a habitat. Explain how living things might interact with them.

_____

_____

12 Why is it important for humans to protect natural habitats?

_____

_____

Certificate of Completion

Congratulations!

_____
(Name)

You have become an expert on habitats!

_____
(signed)

_____
(date)